Contents

1. What IS ISO 17025? 3
2. BENEFITS OF LABORATORY QUALITY MANAGEMENT SYSTEM 4
3. PROCESS OF ACCREDITATION 5
4. SPECIAL FEATURES OF ISO 17025:2017 6
5. IMPARTIALITY (4.1) 7
   EVIDENCES REQUIRED 8
6. CONFIDENTIALITY (4.2) 8
   EVIDENCES REQUIRED 9
7. STRUCTURAL REQUIREMENTS (5.0) 9
   EVIDENCES REQUIRED: 10
8. COMMUNICATION 10
   EVIDENCE REQUIRED 11
9. RESOURCE REQUIREMENT (6.0) 11
10. PERSONNEL (6.2) 11
11. COMPETENCE 13
    EVIDENCES REQUIRED: 14
12. FACILITIES AND ENVIRONMENTAL CONDITION (6.3) 15
    EVIDENCE REQUIRED: 15
13. EQUIPMENT (6.4) 16
    EVIDENCE REQUIRED: 16
    EVIDENCE REQUIRED: 17
14. ELEMENTS OF THE EQUIPMENT 17
    EVIDENCE REQUIRED: 18
15. PROCESS OF CALIBRATION 18
    EVIDENCE REQUIRED: 19
16. METROLOGICAL TRACEABILITY (6.5) 20
   21

	EVIDENCE REQUIRED:	21
17.	EXTERNALLY PROVIDED PRODUCTS AND SERVICE (6.6)	21
	EVIDENCE REQUIRED:	22
18.	PROCESS REQUIREMENT (7.0)	23
19.	REVIEW, REQUEST, TENDERS AND CONTRACTS (7.1)	23
	EVIDENCE REQUIRED:	24
20.	SELECTION, VERIFICATION AND VALIDATION OF METHODS (7.2)	24
	EVIDENCE REQUIRED	26
21.	SAMPLING (7.3)	27
		27
	EVIDENCE REQUIRED	27
22.	HANDLING OF TEST OR CALIBRATION ITEMS (7.4)	28
	EVIDENCE REQUIRED:	29
23.	TECHNICAL RECORD (7.5)	30
	EVIDENCE REQUIRED:	31
24.	EVALUATION OF MEASUREMENT OF UNCERTAINTY (7.6)	31
25.	SOURCES OF MEASUREMENT OF UNCERTAINTY	32
	EVIDENCE REQUIRED:	33
26.	ENSURING THE VALIDITY OF RESULTS (7.7)	33
	EVIDENCE REQUIRED:	34
27.	REPORTING OF RESULTS (7.8)	35
	EVIDENCE REQUIRED:	36
28.	COMPLAINTS (7.9)	37
	EVIDENCE REQUIRED:	38
29.	NON CONFORMING WORK (7.10)	39
	EVIDENCE REQUIRED:	40
30.	CONTROL OF DATA AND INFORMATION MANAGEMENT (7.11)	41
	EVIDENCE REQUIRED:	42
31.	MANAGEMENT SYSTEM DOCUMENTATION (8.2 & 8.3)	43

	EVIDENCE REQUIRED:	44
32.	CONTROL OF RECORDS (8.4)	44
	EVIDENCE REQUIRED:	45
33.	ACTIONS TO ADDRESS THE RISK AND OPPORTUNITY (8.5)	46
	EVIDENCE REQUIRED:	47
34.	IMPROVEMENT (8.6)	47
35.	VARIOUS METHODS FOR IMPROVEMENT	48
36.	ANALYSIS OF DATA FOR CONTINUAL IMPROVEMENT	49
37.	TOOLS USED FOR IMPROVEMENT	49
38.	CORRECTIVE ACTION (8.7)	50
	EVIDENCE REQUIRED:	50
39.	INTERNAL AUDIT (8.8)	50
40.	GUIDELINES FOR CONDUCTION OF INTERNAL AUDIT	51
	EVIDENCE REQUIRED:	52
41.	MANAGEMENT REVIEWS (8.9)	53
	Evidence Required:	54
	Record of:	54

1. What IS ISO 17025?

- ISO/IEC 17025 - ISO standard used for accreditation of testing and calibration laboratories.
- Applicable to all organizations performing tests and/or calibrations.
- ISO/IEC 17025:2017 is applicable regardless of the number of personnel or the extent of the scope.
- Developed by International Organization for Standardization along with international electro technical commission.

- Developed with reference to ISO guide 25.
- First issued in the year 1999.
- Modified in the year 2005.
- Revised on 1st December 2017 as ISO 17025:2017.
- ISO 17025:2017 has 8 clauses while ISO 17025:2005 has 5 clauses.

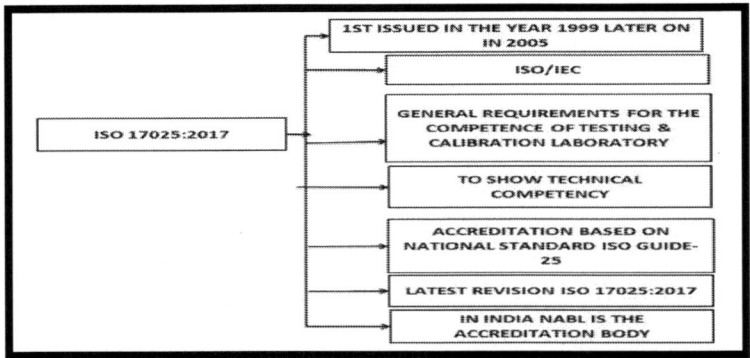

ISO 17025, LABORATORY QUALITY MANAGEMENT SYSTEM

2. BENEFITS OF LABORATORY QUALITY MANAGEMENT SYSTEM

- Continually improves the quality and validity of results.
- Better control on laboratory operation.
- Establishes confidence of management.
- Provide guidelines for the measurement of testing/calibration.
- Better control on the environmental condition.
- Enhances customer confidence.
- Enhances competency of staff.

- Provides greater access to the domestic and international market.
- Saves time and money

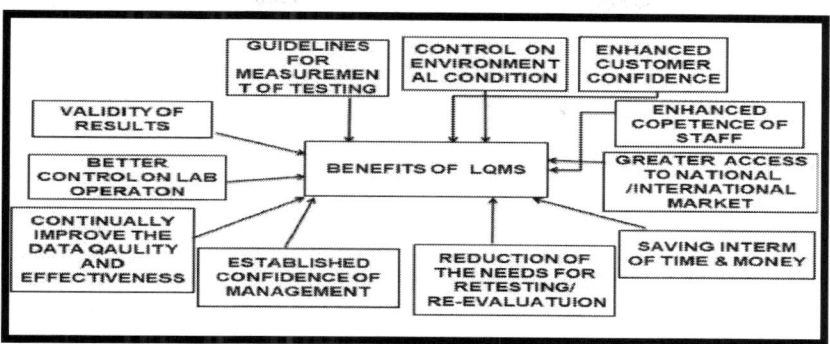

BENEFITS OF ISO 17025:2017

3. PROCESS OF ACCREDITATION

- Accreditation is a third party assessment of laboratory management system to ascertain its capabilities and compliance to ISO17025-2017 requirements.
- Process of accreditation can broadly be broken down in two phases.
    - Phase I: Preparing for application. This involves:
    - Documentation, calibration, training, inter-lab comparison, proficiency testing, internal audit and management review.
- Phase II: Accreditation Audit: This involves:
    - Registration with accreditation body.
    - Adequacy audit and compliances.
    - Stage-I audit and compliances.
    - Stage-II audit and compliances
    - Review by expert committee.
    - Grant of accreditation.

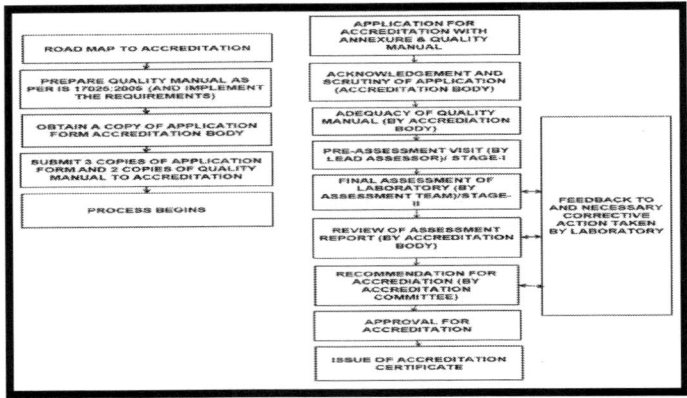

PROCESS OF ACCREDITATION

4. SPECIAL FEATURES OF ISO 17025:2017

- ISO 17025:2017 released on 1st December 2017.
- Risk based thinking in line with ISO 9001:2015 is included.
- Emphasizes more on impartiality and confidentiality as clause- 4.
- Compatible with ISO 9001:2015, Clause gives requirements of quality management system (QMS).
- ISO/IEC 17025:2017 aligned to ISO 9001:2015 principles.
- Follows the new ISO 9001 philosophy:
    - Requires less documented procedures and policies.
    - Focuses more on the outcomes of a process.
    - Quality Manager, Technical Manager and their deputies not required.
    - Emphasis on metrological traceability through clause 6.5.

- Earlier there were 5 clauses in which 4 & 5 were the major clauses.
- Now there are 8 clauses.
- QMS focus on document data control, control of records, internal audit,
  Management review, non- conforming work, corrective action and risk analysis and management.
- For Government laboratories legal identity is not necessary.

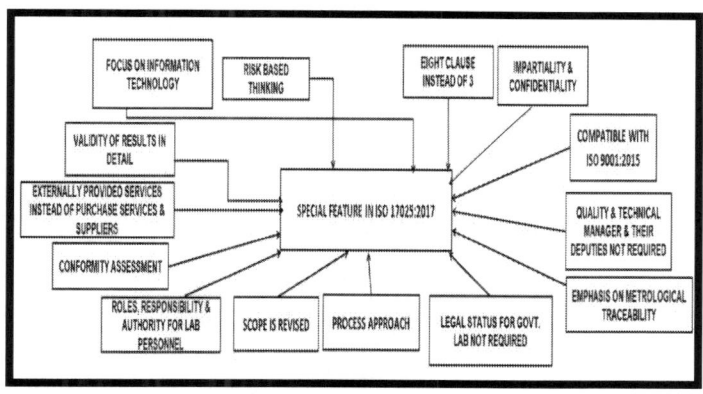

FEATURES OF ISO 17025:2017

5. IMPARTIALITY (4.1)

- Laboratory activities without any bias.
- Without any internal or external influence.
- Responsibility of management.
- Analysis of risk associated with impartiality and the action plan.
- Mechanism to safeguard from internal / external pressure.

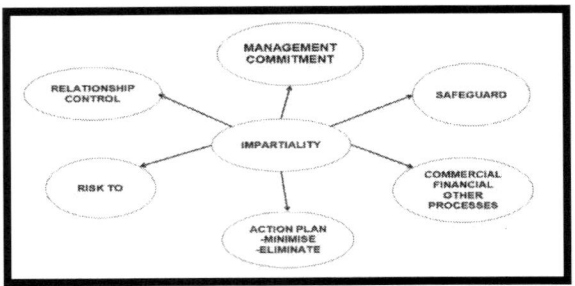

OVERALL CAUSE OF THE IMPARTIALITY AND ITS CONTROL

EVIDENCES REQUIRED

- Establish a procedure to make the laboratory activities impartial.
- Take an oath from the laboratory staff members for the impartiality.
- Provide training on how to be impartial in the laboratory.
- Bar coding of the sample received.
- Restricted access to areas, documents, records.
- Vigilance of the employees and work.
- Investigation and verification of employees at the time of appointment and also in service for their back ground and integrity.
- Implementation of ethical policy.
- Repeat testing of sample in and from outside.
- Analysis of customer complaints & feedback.
- Internal supervision.
- Prevention of mobile photography, data exchange in the laboratory.
- Installation of CCTV cameras.

6. CONFIDENTIALITY (4.2)

- Maintain data and information about the customer, samples, reports, results confidential.
- Information can be shared with code if demanded.
- However should be communicated to the customer unless and until prevented by the court.

- Legal agreement with customer about confidentiality of declaration. This can be in the form of registered affidavit with laboratory about confidentiality and formal letter of confidentiality with customer.
- All those who are associated with laboratory shall maintain confidentiality.

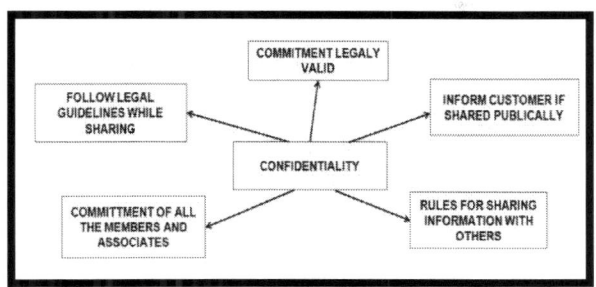

MANAGEMENT OF CONFIDENTIALITY AT WORK PLACE

EVIDENCES REQUIRED

- Declaration from the laboratory staff for the impartiality, confidentiality and Operational Integrity.
- Oath for the impartiality and confidentiality against all the laboratory activities.
    - Establishment of the confidentiality policy.
    - Control on data transfer in laboratory.
- Implementation of ERP system with authorised access.

7. STRUCTURAL REQUIREMENTS (5.0)

- Laboratory to be legal entity.
- Legal status is not mandatory for government organization.
- Any person can be responsible for the system.
- All activities to be considered as per IS 17025:2017.

- Organization chart-specify hierarchy and line of control and communication.
- Define roles, responsibilities and authorities
- Define scope and range of the laboratory activities.
- Define the processes and controls.
- Designate and authorise the personnel for different tasks.
- Maintain records of authorisation.
- Specify policies and procedures.
- Create awareness about the importance of each role.

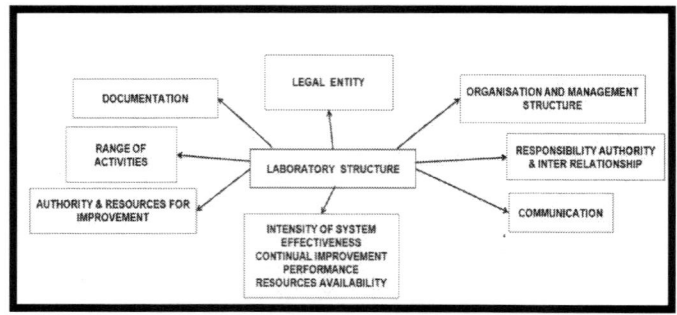

VARIOUS INPUTS FOR THE STRUCTURAL REQUIREMENTS

EVIDENCES REQUIRED:

- Legal identity such as *Gumasta* or shop act.
- Organization chart / structure.
- Established procedures for the management system.
- Appointment letter of person, as a management representative to look after laboratory activities apart from his routine activity.
- Documented roles, responsibility and authority of laboratory staff and management.

- Defines the various methods of communications, such as notice board, internal mail, meetings, management review meeting etc.

8. COMMUNICATION

- Effective internal and external communication:
    - What to communicate?
    - When to communicate?
    - With whom to communicate?
    - How to communicate?
- Communication required with customers, statutory and regulatory bodies, external providers, employees and other interested parties.
- Effective communication reduces the potential problems and resolves the issues.
- Authorisation for important communication required.

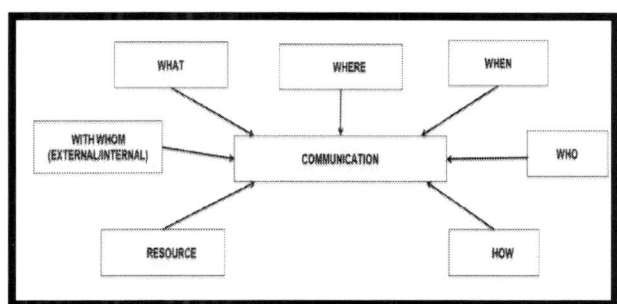

COMMUNICATION

EVIDENCE REQUIRED

- Records of the various internal and external communications:
    - Meetings
    - Circular/notices/penalties/Advertisement
    - Social media apps

- Complaints/feedbacks
- Phone/Mobile/video conferencing
- Training/Seminars/talks
- Visual management
- Audio video aids

9. RESOURCE REQUIREMENT (6.0)

- Major resources required for functioning of the laboratory:
    - Qualified and competent staff.
    - Well maintained equipment.
    - Good layout, infrastructure.
    - Environmental conditions as per requirements.
    - Material and other support.
    - External services as required
- Management responsibilty to estimate and provide the resources.
- Make resources available as and when required and of good quality.
- Monitor and measure the resources.

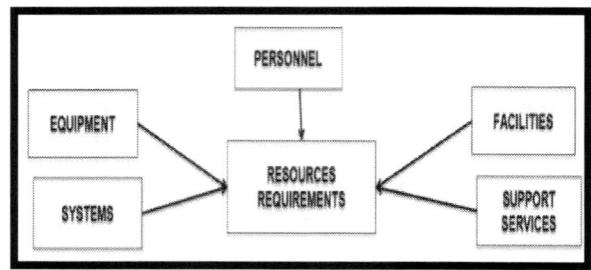

VARIOUS RESOURCES REQUIRED

10. PERSONNEL (6.2)

- Define the competency of the employees.
- Communicate the roles and responsibilities to all.

- Maintain the record of competency, training, supervision, authorization and monitoring of personnel.
- Identify the personnel performing specific laboratory activities.
- Identity the training needs of the personnel.
- Develop training program for the staff members.
- Conduct training program as per the training calendar.
- Trainings can be on job, in-house or external.
- Check the effectiveness of the training provided.
- Create awareness about QMS, Policy, objectives, work processes, job responsibilities.
- Visible efforts to enhance the competency.
- Provide knowledge bank. Build lab knowledge.
- Share the critical incidences. Learn from experience.
- Build a learning environment.
- Create an atmosphere of sharing and learning.
- Periodically check the knowledge of employees.
- Appreciate and reward the employees.

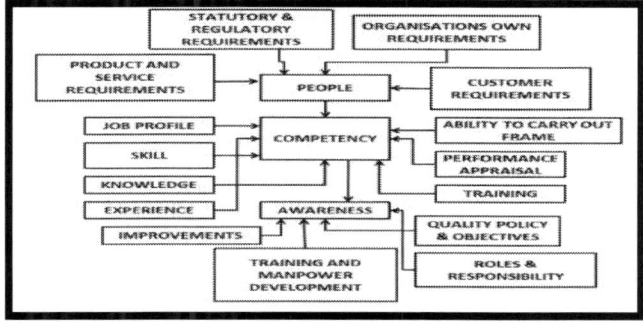

COMPETENCY AND TRAINING

11. COMPETENCE

- Competency is the ability to perform the job in successful way.
- Criteria for competency: education, skills, training and experience for activities, tasks, functions and processes.
- Various ways of building competency of manpower are through:
    - Training.
    - Developing and implementing well designed procedures.
    - Job rotation.
    - Recruiting fully trained people.

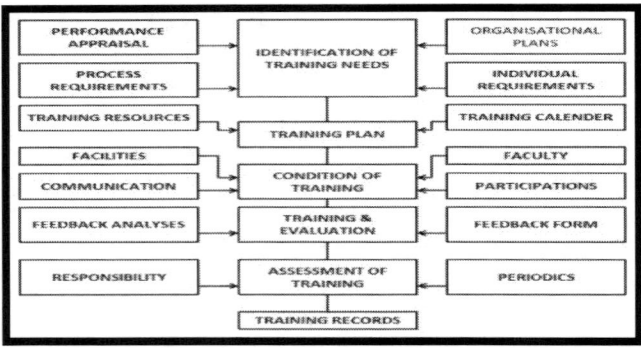

PROCESS OF TRAINING

EVIDENCES REQUIRED:

- List of employees with details of education, experience and training.
- Roles, responsibilities, and authorities assigned.
- Job profile of each task.
- Records of training.
- Competency evaluation record.
- Identification of training needs.

- Training plan for the year (annual training calendar)
- List of training provider (internal/external) institutes.
- List of internal/external training faculties.
- Training attendance record.
- Training feedback.
- Individual training record of laboratory employees.
- Certificate of training received by the individuals.
- Record of effectiveness of training.
- Record of technical training of individual.
- Performance evaluation of individuals.
- Awards/appreciations received by employees.

12. FACILITIES AND ENVIRONMENTAL CONDITION (6.3)

- Design and layout of the lab to provide ease of moment and to avoid interference.
- Environmental conditions affect the laboratory activities.
- **Identify** the various environmental conditions which may affect laboratory activities such as temperature, humidity, radiation, dust, sound, electrical supply, vibration etc.
- Measure and monitor the environmental condition.
- Maintain record of environmental conditions in the lab.

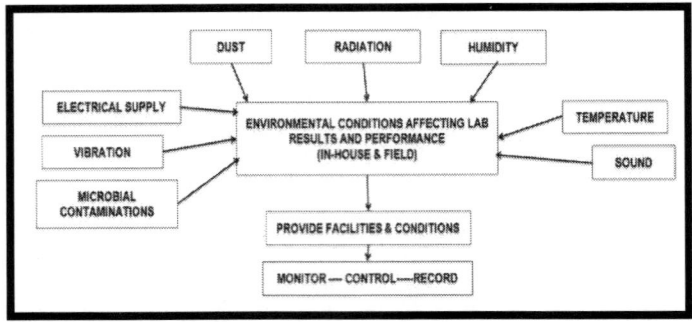

VARIOUS ENVIRONMENTAL CONDITIONS AFFECTING THE LABORATORY ACTIVITIES

EVIDENCE REQUIRED:

- Lay out of the laboratory.
- Environmental condition required for the parameters selected by the laboratory.
- Arrangement to maintain the conditions.
- Environmental monitoring register- record of environmental conditions.
- Housekeeping checklist and its index.
- Responsibility assigned for environmental condition monitoring and housekeeping.

13. EQUIPMENT (6.4)

- Identify the equipments required and used in the laboratory-label these.
- Define range and accuracy desired and available.
- Decide frequency of calibration-internal and external.
- Calibrate the equipment from accredited calibration agency.
- Maintain the frequency of calibration.

- Conduction periodic preventive maintenance of the equipment.
- Provide all the details on the label of the equipment.
- If equipment is not functioning, identify it as "out of service".
- Avoid unintended adjustment of the equipment.
- Maintain equipment history record.
- Have a procedure for handling, transport, storage, use and planned maintenance of the equipment.
- Define the methods of preservation of equipment from environment damage and unauthorized access.
- Define the method of proper functioning of the equipment.

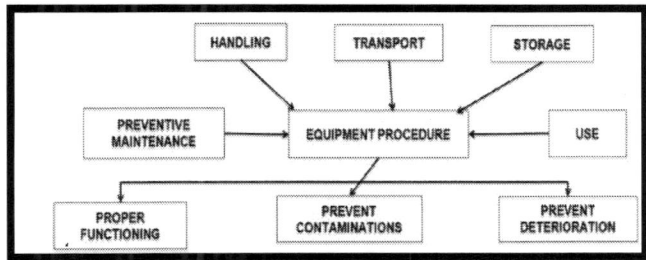

REQUIREMENTS FOR LABORATORY EQUIPMENT

EVIDENCE REQUIRED:

- Equipment label.
  - Name of the equipment.
  - Name of the manufacturer.
  - Identification number.
  - Serial number.
  - Date of calibration.
  - Validity of calibration

- Location of the equipment.
- Frequency of the calibration.
- Type of calibration (internal/external).

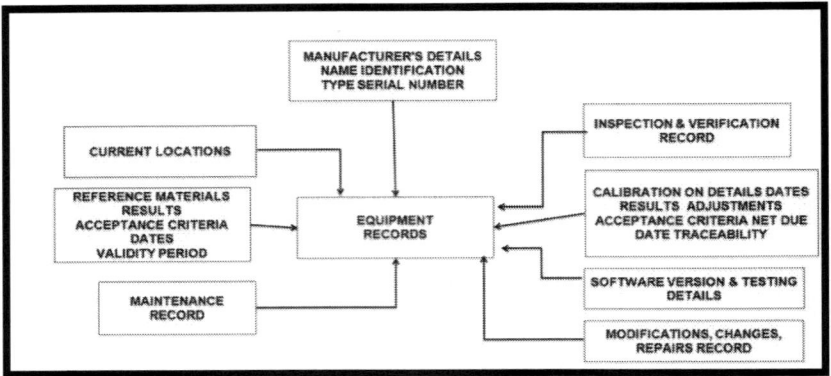

INFORMATION TO BE MAINTAINED FOR THE EQUIPMENT

EVIDENCE REQUIRED:

- List of the equipment and its accessories.
- Label for every equipment including its accessories.
- Preventive and breakdown maintenance records.
- Calibration records.
- Repairs and re-testing records.

14. ELEMENTS OF THE EQUIPMENT

- Measuring instrument.
- Software.
- Measurements standards.
- Reference materials.
- Reference data.
- Accuracy of the equipment.
- Calibration of equipment.

- Reagents and consumables.

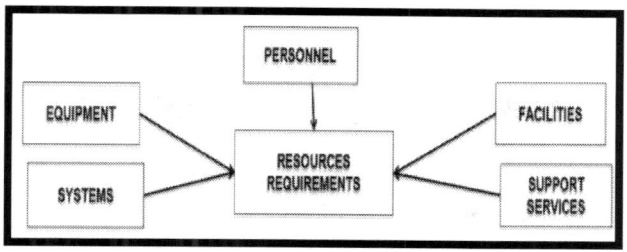

ELEMENTS OF THE EQUIPMENT

EVIDENCE REQUIRED:

- Record of:
  - Equipments and its accessories
  - List of reference materials
  - Reference data.
  - Equipment maintenance.
  - Software validation.
  - Calibration.
  - Auxiliary and apparatus used.
  - Consumables and reagent

15. PROCESS OF CALIBRATION

Calibration is the activity of verifying, by comparison with a standard, the accuracy of a measuring instrument of any type. It may also include adjustment of the instrument to bring it into alignment with the standard.

- Identify the equipment to be calibrated.
- Collect the information about use of the equipment.
- Decide the frequency of calibration
- Internal and external calibration.

- Search for the competent calibration laboratory.
- Check the scope of the calibration laboratory.
- Ensure that the validity of the accreditation of the calibration agency.
- Check if the agency is accredited as per ISO 17025:2017.
- Check the traceability certification of the calibration agency.
- Define the specification of the equipment to be calibrated.
- Make sure that the equipment is transported safely.
- After calibration check the calibration certificate.
- Check whether the measurement of uncertainty provided.
- Check the measurement of uncertainty is acceptable to the laboratory.
- Verify the traceability certificate.
- Ensure proper calibration label is pasted on the equipment.
- If equipment is out of calibration, make sure that the testing/calibration is not carried out using the equipment.
- Mark the out of calibration equipments.
- Maintain the details of calibration

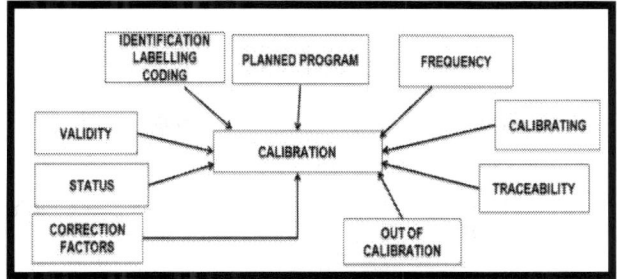

PROCESS OF CALIBRATION

EVIDENCE REQUIRED:

- List of equipment.
- Calibration plan with details of frequency of equipment used in the laboratory.
- Preventive maintenance checklist for every equipment.
- Equipment maintenance history record.
- List of calibration agencies.
- Scope of calibration agency.
- Calibration certificate.
- Record of review and verification of calibration certificate.
- Records of traceability.
- Records of measurement of uncertainty.
- Record of equipment "out of calibration".

16. METROLOGICAL TRACEABILITY (6.5)

- Metrological traceability is defined as "the property of a measurement result whereby the result can be related to a reference through a documented unbroken chain of

calibrations, each contributing to the measurement uncertainty
- Terms and terminology related to measurement traceability concept.
- Establishing metrological traceability.
- Demonstrating metrological traceability.
- Laboratory needs to establish and maintain metrological traceability of its results.
- Measurement result of the laboratory needs to be traceable to SI units.
- Measurement traceability can be achieved through:
    - Reliable and accurate measurements
    - Calibration. High accuracy instrument require more frequent calibration.
    - Software validation
    - Properly safeguarding the instrument
    - Accurate recording of the results
    - Traceability of calibration to national and international reference standards.
    - Verification of traceability certificate.

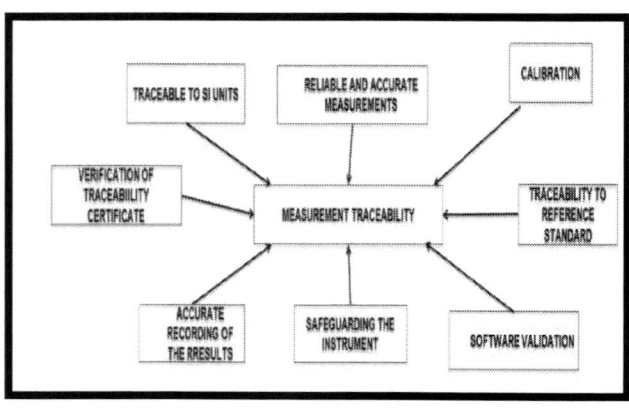

MEASUREMENT TRACEABILITY

EVIDENCE REQUIRED:

- Calibration certificate.
- Verification of calibration certificate.
- Traceability certificate.
- Certificate with values of certified reference material.

17. EXTERNALLY PROVIDED PRODUCTS AND SERVICE (6.6)

- External providers are the suppliers who provide material or service such as calibration, testing, maintenance, housekeeping etc. eg. Calibration, participation in Inter laboratory comparison or in proficiency testing, purchase of equipment, consumable, reagent, glass wares, subcontracting of laboratory.
- Selection of external providers
- Clarity in the product and service requirement.
- Clarity in terms and conditions.
- Define acceptance criteria.
- Evaluation of external providers.
- Selection of external providers.
- Performance evaluation.
- Monitoring of external providers.
- Re-evaluation of external providers.
- Provide necessary and adequate information to the external provider.
- Specify the product and services needed.

- Review the requirement.
- Product or services are as per the defined specifications.

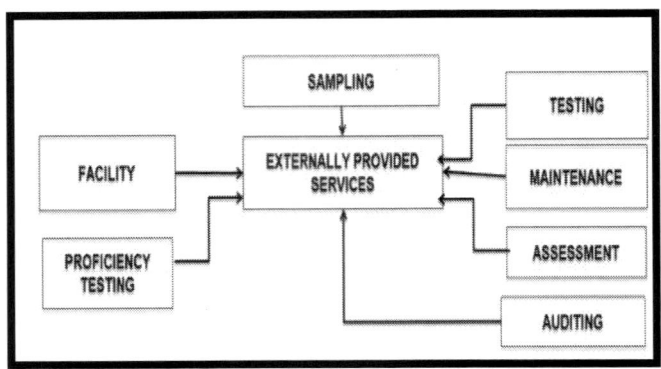

EXTERNAL SERVICES USE

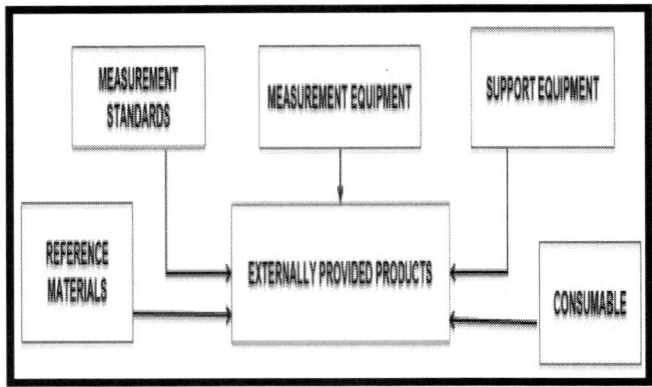

VARIOUS EXTERNALLY PROVIDED PRODUCT

EVIDENCE REQUIRED:

- List of externally providers (supplier and service providers).
- Evaluation of external providers.
- List of critical consumables.
- Material inspection record.
- Specification of material.
- Purchase order.

18. PROCESS REQUIREMENT (7.0)

- Customer requirement analysis.
- Method verification and validation.
- Lab processes. Testing/calibration.
- Quality Assurance.
- Measurement of uncertainty.
- Sampling.
- Handling of test item.
- Technical records.
- Report preparation.
- Handling complaints and non-conforming work.
- Lab information management system.

19. REVIEW, REQUEST, TENDERS AND CONTRACTS (7.1)

- Review request, tenders and contracts considering:
    - The requirements.
    - Capability and resource availability.
    - Method and procedures.
    - Inform customer if requirements are inappropriate.
    - Resolved the deviation.
    - Inform customer for any deviation.
    - Clarify and confirm with customer.
    - Resolve queries and disputes.
- Complaints

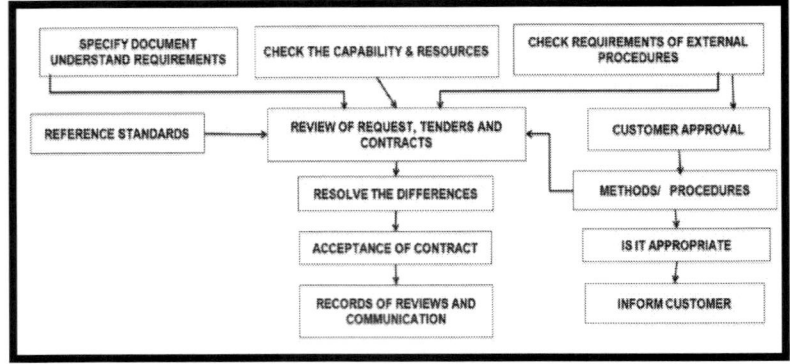

REVIEW, REQUEST, TENDERS AND CONTRACTS

EVIDENCE REQUIRED:

- Develop procedure for review of requests, tenders and contracts.
- Maintain review request form.
- Review of customer requirement.
- Record of amendments and communication.
- Customer approvals of external providers, if any.
- Methods and statement of confirmation.
- Customer visit report.
- Communication log.

20. SELECTION, VERIFICATION AND VALIDATION OF METHODS (7.2)

- Refer the latest valid edition of standard.
- Additional information supporting the standard method
- Capability to verify test methods.
- Customer approval.
- Method appropriateness.

- Maintained updated documents such as manuals, procedures, and work instructions.
- Authorized person for maintaining documents.
- Validation of methods for non-standard method.
- Inform customer if any non-validated method used.
- Verify the methods used.

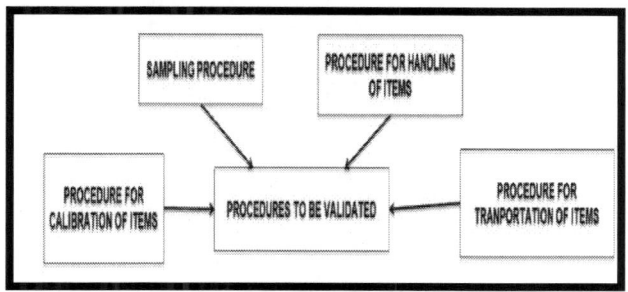

PROCESS OF VALIDATION

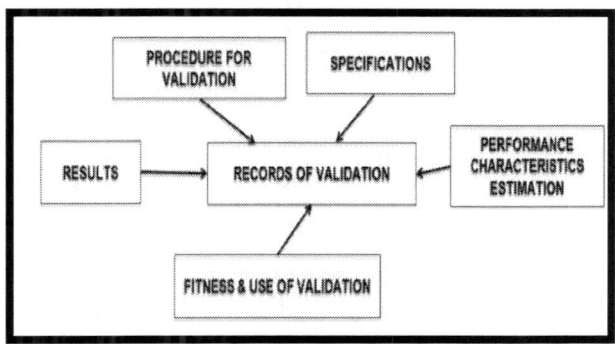

RECORDS REQUIRED FOR VALIDATION

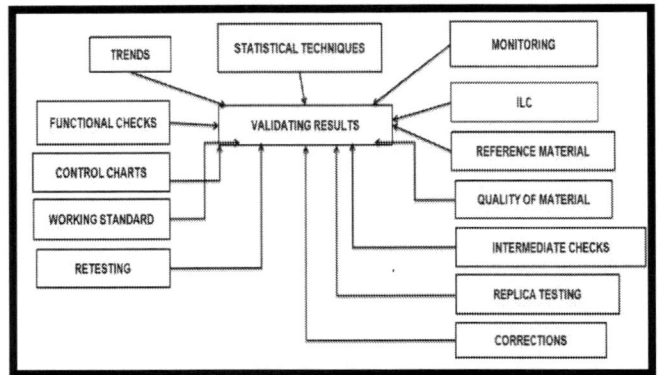

MECHANISM OF VALIDATING THE RESULTS

EVIDENCE REQUIRED

- List of international/national standards used.
- Developed procedure for validation.
- Maintain Records of:
    - Customer approval of the methods.
    - Verification of the methods to achieve the required performance.
    - Validation of methods carried out, if any.
    - Change in validation methods.
    - Performance characteristics of any validated or change of validation methods.
    - Specification of the requirements.
    - Results obtained from validated methods.
    - Fitness of use for the intended purpose.

21. SAMPLING (7.3)

SAMPLING METHOD

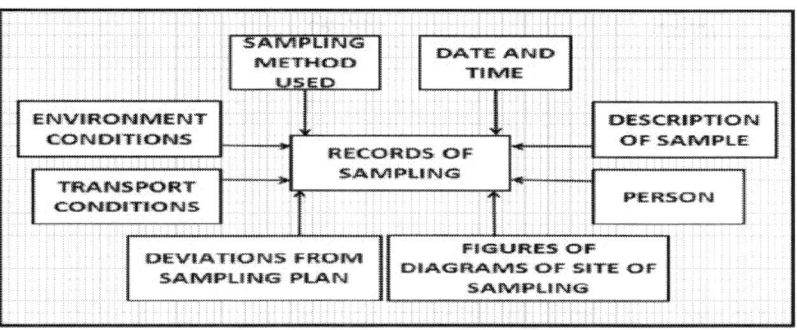

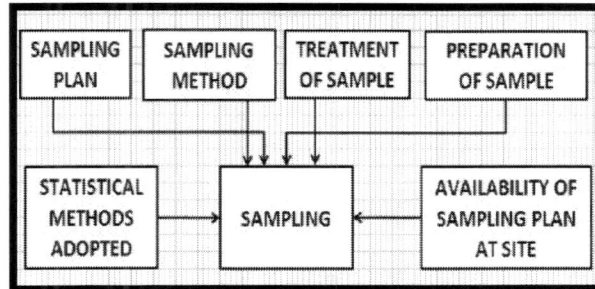

EVIDENCE REQUIRED

- Type, number, size and quantity of sample collected.
- Location of sample.
- Source/site conditions.
- Equipments/container used.
- Preservatives used.
- Labels and documents required.
- Time of sampling.
- Time for which the sample is to be preserved.
- Sampling plan.
- Sampling authorizations- for example, important in case of joint sampling.
- Client name and contact information.

- Safety precautions during sampling.
- Training records of the person conducting sampling.
- Authorization of person conducting sampling.
- Records of environmental condition during sampling.
- Record of conditions to be maintained during transportation of sample.

22. HANDLING OF TEST OR CALIBRATION ITEMS (7.4)

- Establish procedure for:
    - Transportation,
    - Receipt,
    - Handling,
    - Protection,
    - Storage,
    - Retention, and
    - Disposal or return.
- Precaution to be taken to avoid the loss of the sample during handling.
    - Handling instruction to be defined.
    - No ambiguity in sample identification.
    - Criteria for sample acceptance.

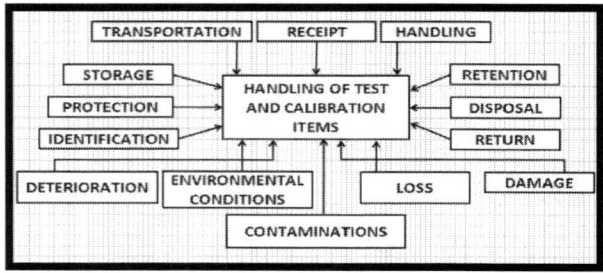

HANDLING OF TESTING AND CALIBRATION ITEMS

EVIDENCE REQUIRED:

- Procedure for the transportation, receipt, handling, protection, storage, retention and / or disposal of test items.
- Records of environmental condition at storage.
- Record of disposal.
- Receipt register.
- Criteria for sample acceptance (test/calibration item).
- Record of environmental condition for maintaining for the storage of test and calibration item.
- Condition of sample.
- Packaging of the sample.
- Labelling of the sample.
- Quantity of the sample.
- Signature of the authorized person.
- Proper seal on the bottle.
- Proper coat on the bottle.
- Letter addressing the parameters to be tested/calibrated.

23. TECHNICAL RECORD (7.5)

Technical records are the records which are being generated during the analysis such as testing, receipt, calibration, measurement of uncertainty, validity of results, meteorological traceability etc.

- Keep all the technical record affecting the measurement of results.
- Specify the time and the identity.
- Maintain original observation and data.
- Person responsible for each laboratory activity.

- Amendment to technical records- previous and latest version.
- Identify the person making the amendment on technical records.
- The technical records can be is maintained in soft or hard copy.
- Evidence required.
    - Technical records can be in the form of log sheet, work sheet, check sheet, forms, graphs, contracts, agreement, notes, reports, customer communications, feedback, reviews, photographs etc.
    - Responsibility, authority for preparation and maintenance of record.
    - Unique identification number.
    - The date and time when the records are prepared.
    - Legibility and traceability of records.
    - Authority for review and approval of records.
    - Traceability to specific task.
    - Storage, retention and preservation of records.

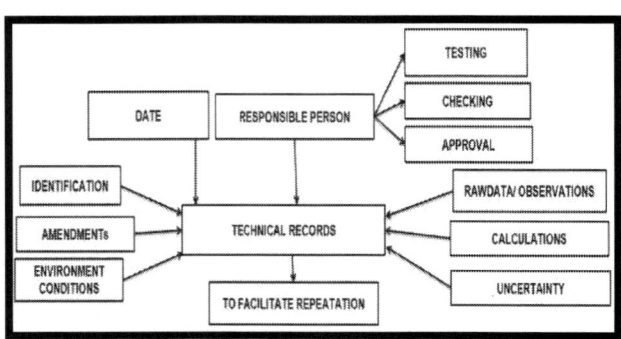

VARIOUS TECHNICAL RECORDS

EVIDENCE REQUIRED:

- List of technical records maintained by the laboratory.
- Procedure for making the correction in technical records.
- Methods of making correction in technical record.
- Appointment of the person who can make correction in technical records.
- Maintain following technical records.
    - Calibration
    - Sampling
    - Inter laboratory comparison
    - Test reports
    - Receipt records
    - Raw data records
    - MU calculations records
    - Z score calculation
    - Proficiency testing record
    - Retesting of retained record
    - Intermediate checks record, Software validation records, etc

24. EVALUATION OF MEASUREMENT OF UNCERTAINTY (7.6)

Uncertainty is a quantification of the doubt about the measurement result. There are various factors which contributes the uncertainty of measurement.

- Identify the sources for measurement of uncertainty

- Calculate the measurement of uncertainty for all calibrations.
- Evaluation of measurement of uncertainty.

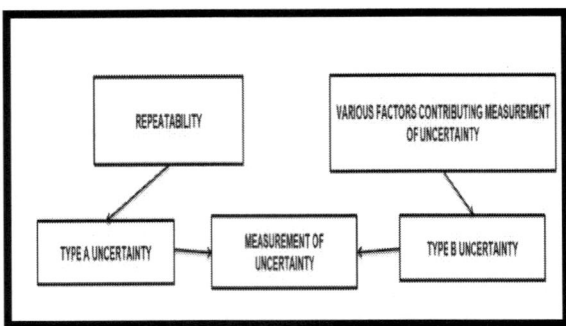

TYPES OF MEASUREMENT OF UNCERTAINTY

25. SOURCES OF MEASUREMENT OF UNCERTAINTY

- Various sources of Measurement of Uncertainty are:
  - Incomplete definition of measurand.
  - Calibration
  - Sampling.
  - Storage and handling condition
  - Methods/procedure.
  - Instrument effect.
  - Equipment
  - Measurement condition.
  - Environmental condition.
  - Random effect.
  - Computational effect.
  - Reference value.
  - Blank correction.
  - Operator effect.
  - Customer requirements.

  Process of Uncertainty measurement:

- Define various terminologies used in the measurement of uncertainty.

- Establish the procedure for the measurement of uncertainty.
- Provide technical training on calculations of measurement uncertainty to technical staff.
- Conduct repeatability for type A uncertainty.
- Keep records of all the calibration certificate of the equipment used in testing/calibration.
- Keep the records of the certified reference material used.
- Calculate type B uncertainty.
- Calculate expanded uncertainty.
- Keep the record of the measurement uncertainty calculation along with uncertainty budget.

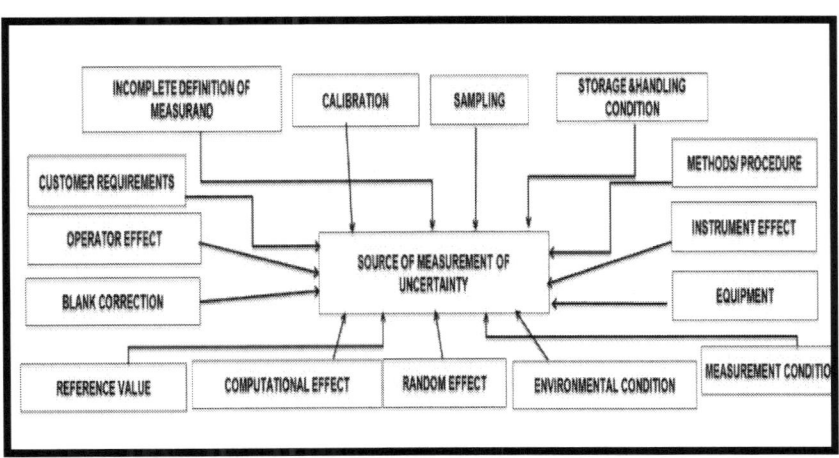

SOURCES OF MEASUREMENT OF UNCERTAINTY

EVIDENCE REQUIRED:

- Calibration of equipments
- Traceability of certified reference material

- Repeatability data
- Calculations of Uncertainty measurement

26. ENSURING THE VALIDITY OF RESULTS (7.7)

- This is Quality Assurance of the laboratory processes.
- Use of reference material or quality control materials
- Conducting intermediate checks on measuring equipments.
- Retesting or recalibration of retained items.
- Replicate test or calibration using the same or different methods.
- Periodic checking of measuring and test equipment
- Use of alternative equipment
- Use of correlation between different characteristics of an item
- Participate in inter laboratory comparisons
- Participate in proficiency testing.
- Statistical analysis of data for trend estimation.

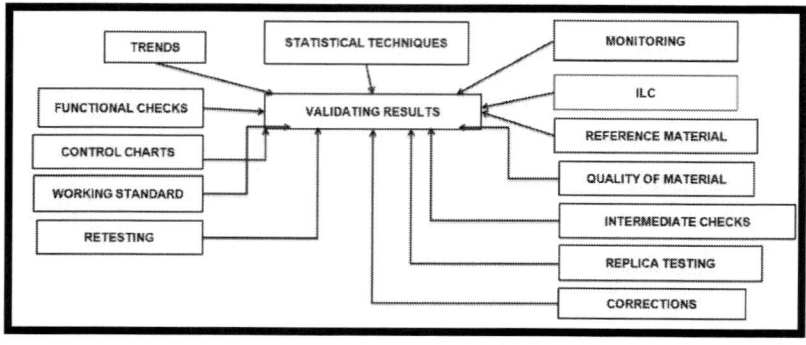

PROCESS OF VALIDATING RESULTS:

EVIDENCE REQUIRED:

- Established procedure for monitoring the validity of results.
- Retesting for all the parameters.
- Functional checks carried out.
- Working standards with control charts.
- Intermediate checks carried out.
- Replica testing and analysis.
- Retesting of retained or recalibration items.
- Statistical analysis carried out.
- Results of Inter-laboratory carried out.
- Inter-laboratory comparison plan.
- Z score for all the parameters.
- Plan for Inter-laboratory comparison and proficiency testing.
- Proficiency testing results and analysis.
- Testing of blind sample.
- Records of document control, internal audit, management review, monitoring and measurement, calibration etc.

27. REPORTING OF RESULTS (7.8)

Lab reports are used for decision making.

- Requirement for the preparation of final report.
- Report should be meaningful, easy to interpret and traceable.
- Clear and unambiguous report with all details.

- Specific requirement for test report to be ensured.
- Specific requirement for calibration certificate to be fulfilled.
- Reporting requirement related to sampling.
- Decision rules related to conformity statement and report.
- Reporting requirement related to opinion and interpretation.
- Follow method of amending the report. Don't over write.
- Maintain the signature of authorised person.

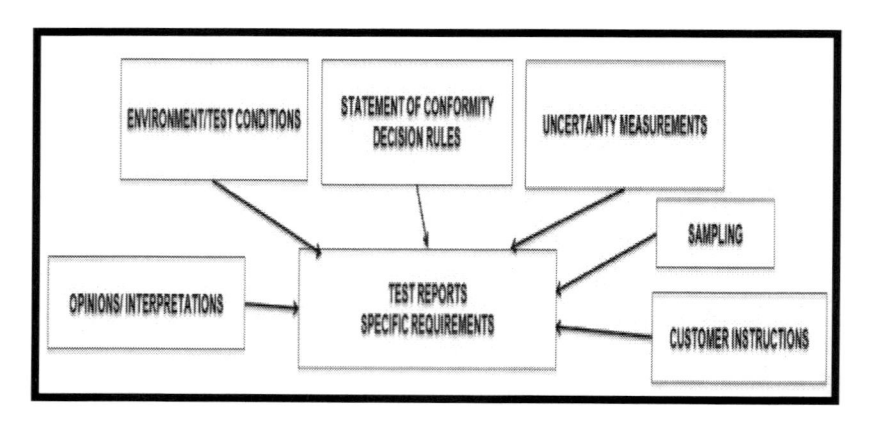

SPECIFIC REQUIREMENTS FOR TEST REPORTS

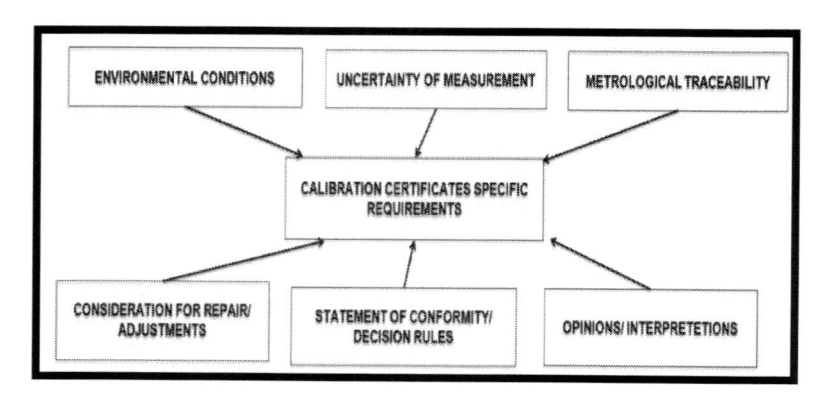

SPECIFIC REQUIREMENT FOR THE CALIBRATION CERTIFICATE

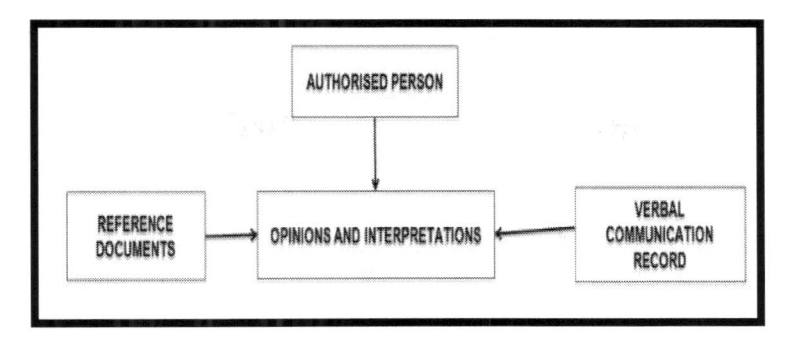

```
          ┌─────────────────┐
          │ AUTHORISED PERSON│
          └────────┬────────┘
                   ▼
┌──────────┐   ┌──────────────┐   ┌──────────────┐
│ REFERENCE│──▶│ OPINIONS AND │◀──│    VERBAL    │
│ DOCUMENTS│   │INTERPRETATIONS│   │COMMUNICATION │
└──────────┘   └──────────────┘   │    RECORD    │
                                  └──────────────┘
```

OPINION AND INTERPRETATION

EVIDENCE REQUIRED:

- Test report or calibration certificate.
- Interpretation of test/calibration results.
- List of persons making opinion and interpretation.
- Details of experience, education, scientific knowledge of the person making opinion and interpretation.
- Records of amendment of report.
- Person making the report.
- Person authorizing and approving reports.
- Identification for test/calibration report.
- Identification of corrected report after amendment.
- Record of the analysis on which reports are made.
- Details of statement of conformity as per decision rules.
- Sampling details.
- Details of measurement of uncertainty.
- Details of repairs or any adjustment in equipment.
- Details of any specific methods, authorities and customer.

28. COMPLAINTS (7.9)

- Customer is most important for the survival and growth of the lab. Therefore, customer complaints as well as the complaints of interested parties need to be handled immediately.
- Prepare a detail process for-
    - Receiving,
    - Validating,
    - Investigating the complaint and
    - Actions needed to resolve the same.
- Maintain the record of complaints, its tracking and actions taken to resolve it.
- Ensure that proper consultation is done.
- Responsibility of the laboratory for management of complaint handling and resolution.
- Acknowledge the receipt of the complaint.
- Keep complainant communication.

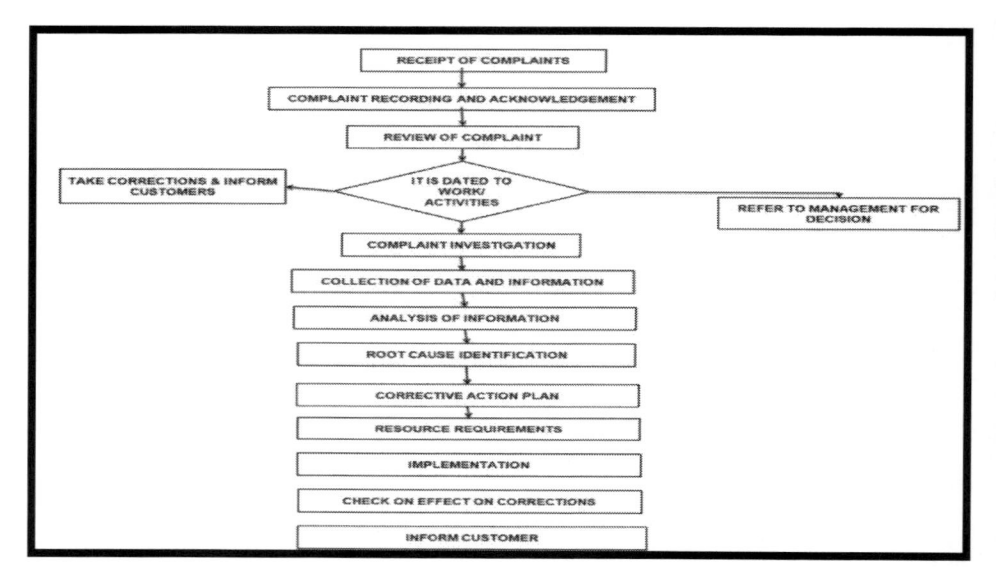

```
RECEIPT OF COMPLAINTS
        ↓
COMPLAINT RECORDING AND ACKNOWLEDGEMENT
        ↓
REVIEW OF COMPLAINT
        ↓
IT IS DATED TO WORK/ACTIVITIES
   ↙         ↘
TAKE CORRECTIONS    REFER TO MANAGEMENT
& INFORM CUSTOMERS      FOR DECISION
        ↓
COMPLAINT INVESTIGATION
        ↓
COLLECTION OF DATA AND INFORMATION
        ↓
ANALYSIS OF INFORMATION
        ↓
ROOT CAUSE IDENTIFICATION
        ↓
CORRECTIVE ACTION PLAN
        ↓
RESOURCE REQUIREMENTS
        ↓
IMPLEMENTATION
        ↓
CHECK ON EFFECT ON CORRECTIONS
        ↓
INFORM CUSTOMER
```

- **PROCESS OF COMPLAINT SUMMARY**

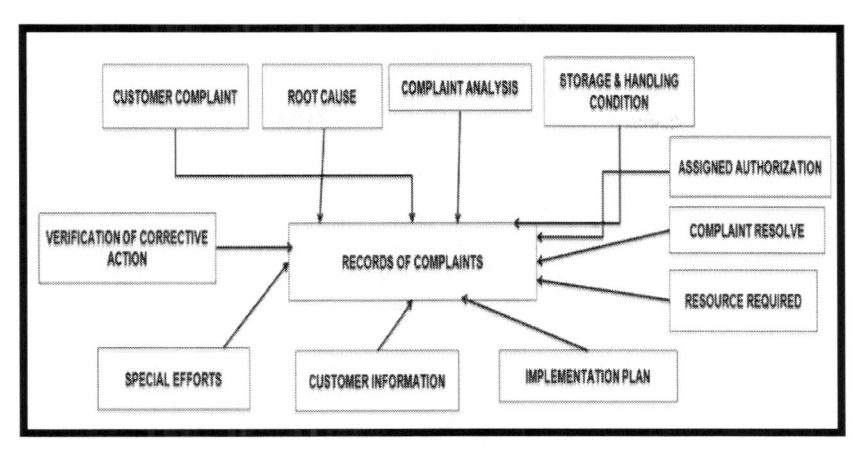

```
[CUSTOMER COMPLAINT]  [ROOT CAUSE]  [COMPLAINT ANALYSIS]  [STORAGE & HANDLING CONDITION]
                                                          [ASSIGNED AUTHORIZATION]
[VERIFICATION OF CORRECTIVE ACTION] → [RECORDS OF COMPLAINTS] ← [COMPLAINT RESOLVE]
                                                               [RESOURCE REQUIRED]
[SPECIAL EFFORTS]  [CUSTOMER INFORMATION]  [IMPLEMENTATION PLAN]
```

RECORDS OF COMPLAINTS

EVIDENCE REQUIRED:

- Various documented information needed related to the complaints are:

    - Procedure for complaint handling
    - Customer complaints.
    - Root cause analysis about every complaint.
    - Analysis carried out on complaints.
    - Person responsible for handling complaints.
    - Resolve of complaint.
    - Corrective action plan.
    - Resource required for taking corrective actions.
    - Customer information.
- Implementation plan of the corrective action taken.
- Any special effort taken to resolve the complaint.
- Verification records of the corrective action.

29. NON CONFORMING WORK (7.10)

Non-conformity is a condition that does not conform to the requirements/specifications of the prescribed work.

The various non-conforming works are:

- Sample not collected properly.
- Sample not labelled properly.
- Sample not stored in correct way.
- Conditions while transportation not followed.
- The test procedure not followed.
- Equipment checks not carried out.
- Unauthorised person carrying out the work in the lab.
- Training to the persons not provided.
- Safety precautions during testing not followed.
- Calibration of equipments not carried out.
- Required documents not available at a point of use.
- Records are not maintained.
- Raw data books, forms and formats, log books, registers not updated. Signatures missing.
- Test calibration reports not as per the requirement.
- Reports are illegible or send to wrong location.
- Environmental conditions during testing not monitored.
- The data information and confidentiality not maintained.
- Unauthorised person accessing the information.
  - ➢ The non-conforming work affects the laboratory performance, reputation.

- When a non-conforming work is detected, then it needs to be recorded immediately and brought to the notice of the authorized person.
- The authorized person has to decide the actions required on the non-conforming work.
- The authorized person to make a decision about the acceptability.
- Recall the test/calibration report if non-conformity observed after report is issued.
- Authorized the resumption of work after non-conformity.
- Define the roles and responsibilities for the management of non- conforming work.
- The non-conforming work needs to be analysed for root cause for preventing the recurrence of the same.

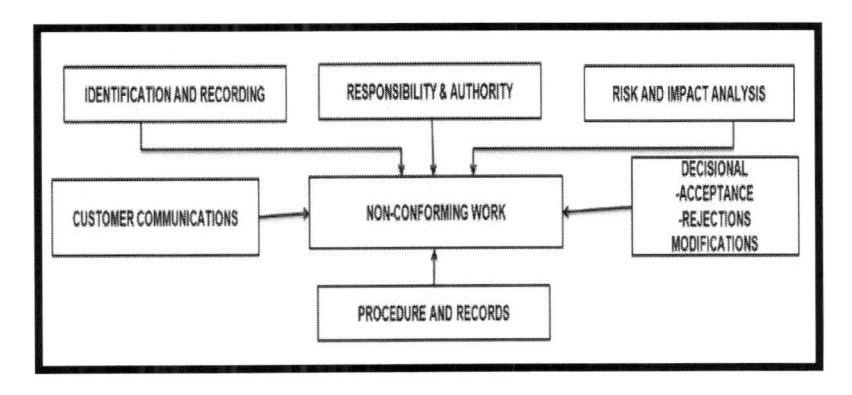

MECHANISM OF NON-CONFORMING ACTIVITY

EVIDENCE REQUIRED:

- Established procedure for non-conforming work.
- Defined roles and responsibilities for the management of non-conforming work.

- Maintain the following records for the non-conforming work:
  - Identification of non-conformance.
  - Root cause analysis.
  - Corrective action and effectiveness of the actions.
  - Impact analysis on previous results.
  - Customer information.
  - Evaluation of the corrective action taken against non-conforming work.

30. CONTROL OF DATA AND INFORMATION MANAGEMENT (7.11)

Information management system is needed for:

- Collecting.
- Processing.
- Recording.
- Reporting.
- Storing and
- Analysing the data and the information for planning the strategies and improvements.

Plan and develop the information management system in order to:

- Achieve easy accessibility of data and information.
- Enhance accuracy and timeliness.
- Achieve ease of reporting.
- Reduce errors.
- Realize better retrieval of data and information.

- Prepare detailed and legible reports.
- Ensure access controls.
- Ensure easy tracking and analysis of data and trends.
- Ensure traceability of reports.
- Integrate with other systems.
- Securely store and transmit electronic data.
- Protect from unintended or unauthorized access.
- Check calculation and data transfer.

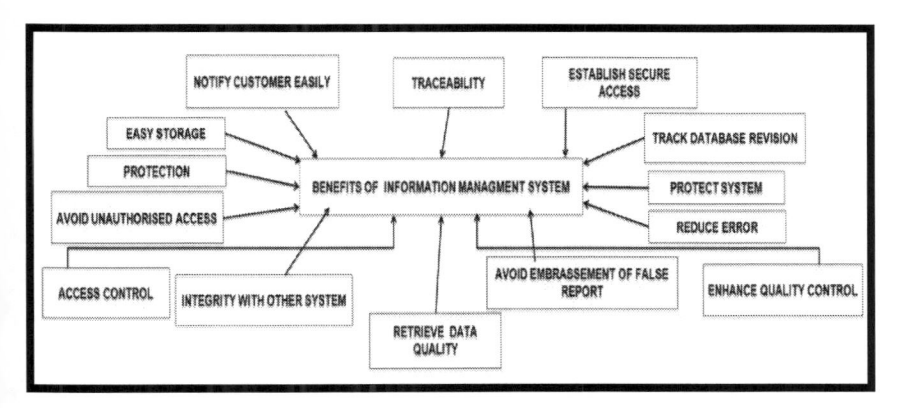

BENEFITS OF LABORATORY INFORMATION MANAGEMENT SYSTEM

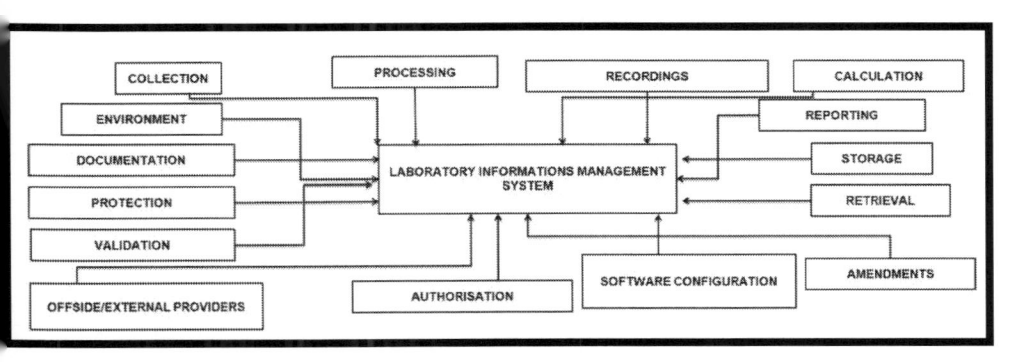

LABORATORY INFORMATION MANAGEMENT SYSTEM

EVIDENCE REQUIRED:

- Process of data as well as information management system to be defined.

- Define the authority for the access of data.
- Records of incidences of system failure and corrective actions taken.
- Authorisation for MIS.
- Validation mechanism of laboratory information management system.
- Software configuration.
- Deviation, if any, and actions taken.
- Corrective action.
- Modified procedures and systems.

31. MANAGEMENT SYSTEM DOCUMENTATION (8.2 & 8.3)

Any instruction, guidelines, procedure, works instruction which is required for performing a particular task is called document. Documents are used for information, and also for further planning/analysis/decision making.

Documented information can be any of the following type:

- Soft or hard,
- Paper,
- Manuals or books,
- Drawing or picture,
- Instructions,
- Circulars,
- Notes,

- Agreements,
- Presentations,
- Electronic software applications
- Programmes or photographs etc.

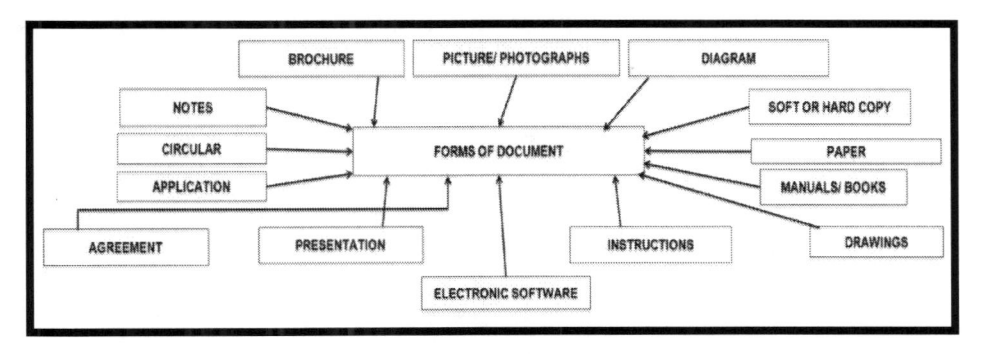

```
                BROCHURE    PICTURE/PHOTOGRAPHS    DIAGRAM
       NOTES                                              SOFT OR HARD COPY
       CIRCULAR            FORMS OF DOCUMENT              PAPER
       APPLICATION                                        MANUALS/BOOKS
  AGREEMENT       PRESENTATION        INSTRUCTIONS        DRAWINGS
                        ELECTRONIC SOFTWARE
```

FORMS OF DOCUMENT

Various controls on documents are:

- Prepare and review the document with proper authorization.
- Provide identification number.
- Make sure that the latest version of documents is available at a point of use.
- Prepare document distribution list.
- Follow the revision mechanism.
- Control access to documents.
- Control on obsolete documents.
- Suitability for use.

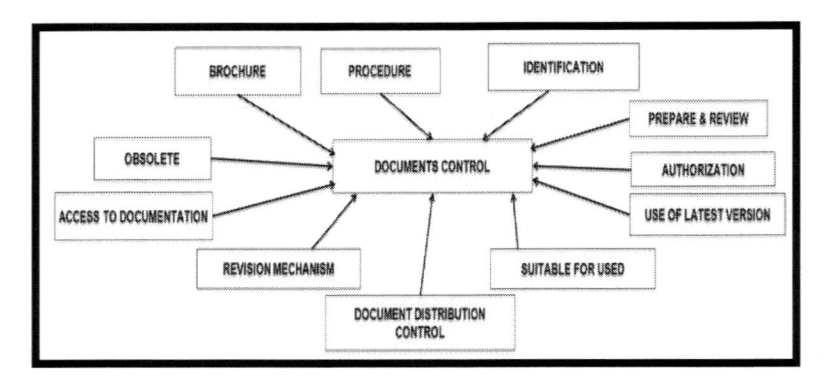

DOCUMENT CONTROL

EVIDENCE REQUIRED:

- Establish procedure for document data control.
- Maintain master list of documents.
- List of external origin documents.
- List of manuals used in the laboratory.
- List of records, formats used.
- Document change note.
- Document approval.
- Record of distribution of documents and format.
- List of work instruction, technical procedure, layout, diagram, photographs, hard or soft copies.

32. CONTROL OF RECORDS (8.4)

Records are the type of documents which gives the information about the happening of past. Laboratory is required maintain the records as an evidence during legal or audit process.

- Establish records for fulfilment.
- Defines the various control of records such as:
    - Identification.
    - Storage.

- Protection.
- Back-up.
- Archive.
- Retrieval.
- Retention time and
- Disposal of records.
- Retain records as per agreed terms and legal requirements.
- Access to records to be defined.
- Make available as required.
- Don't alter or modify the records.

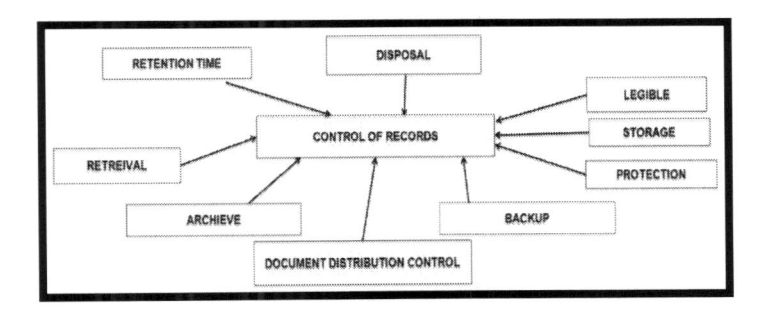

```
                RETENTION TIME        DISPOSAL
                                                      LEGIBLE
                            CONTROL OF RECORDS        STORAGE
        RETREIVAL                                     PROTECTION
                    ARCHIEVE              BACKUP
                        DOCUMENT DISTRIBUTION CONTROL
```

CONTROL OF RECORDS

EVIDENCE REQUIRED:

- List of master list of records to be maintained.
- Records for all laboratory activities to be maintained such as:
    - Receipt register,
    - Environmental monitoring register,
    - Staff details,
    - Training, competence, training attendance, effectiveness etc.

- Equipments, calibration, preventive maintenance etc.
- Sampling details,
- Meteorological traceability.
- Review, requests, tenders and contracts.
- Various quality assurance records etc.
- External providers performance.
- Specification of material,
- Risk and opportunities and its mitigation.
- Internal audit.
- Management review meeting.
- Compliance to legal requirement.
- Improvements planned and achieved.
- Customer feedback and complaints. Actions on these.
- Corrective action.
- QMS activities.

33. ACTIONS TO ADDRESS THE RISK AND OPPORTUNITY (8.5)

Risk is the uncertainty in carrying out the work while opportunity is the exploration of new initiative.

- Establish and implement the procedure for risk and opportunities.
- Define the risks and opportunities in processes and operation of laboratory.
- Carry out SWOT analysis.
- Brainstorm for prioritizing the risk and opportunity.
- Plan the actions to mitigate the risk and opportunities.

- Form the team to implement the actions.
- Train the team.
- Brainstorm the operational controls or improvement actions.
- Finalize the controls or improvement actions
- Plan to execute the controls or improvement actions.
- Execute the controls or improvement actions.
- Evaluate the effectiveness of control or improvement actions by re-assessing the risk.

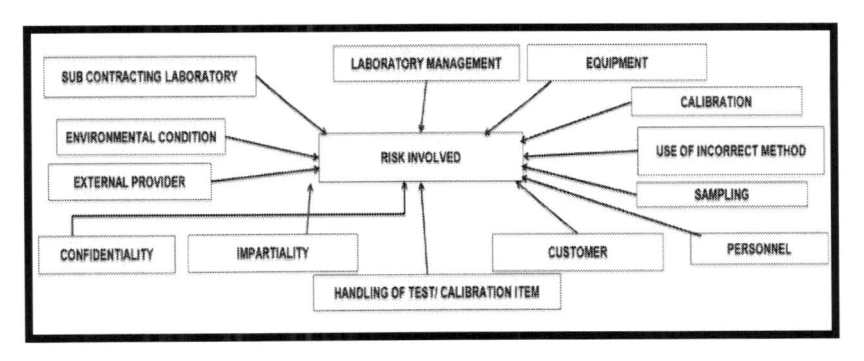

![Risk Assessment Diagram showing RISK INVOLVED connected to: SUB CONTRACTING LABORATORY, LABORATORY MANAGEMENT, EQUIPMENT, CALIBRATION, ENVIRONMENTAL CONDITION, USE OF INCORRECT METHOD, EXTERNAL PROVIDER, SAMPLING, CONFIDENTIALITY, IMPARTIALITY, CUSTOMER, PERSONNEL, HANDLING OF TEST/ CALIBRATION ITEM]

RISK ASSESSMENT

EVIDENCE REQUIRED:

Records of:

- Risk analysis.
- Action taken against each identified risk.
- Improvements as per risk management.
- Personnel authorized for the work.

34. IMPROVEMENT (8.6)

The continual improvement process can be conducted by:

- Significant breakthrough projects.
- Small-step on going improvement activities.

Improvement areas are:

- External provider services, internal audit, training and competence of staff, utilization of laboratory equipments, metrological traceability, impartiality, confidentiality, retesting of retained item, retesting, Interlaboratory comparison, proficiency testing, calibration of laboratory equipment, internal audit etc.
- Results of samples, process and audits.
- Communications –internal and external.
- Management information system.
- Process controls and effectiveness.
- Resources optimization.
- Technology modification and up gradation.

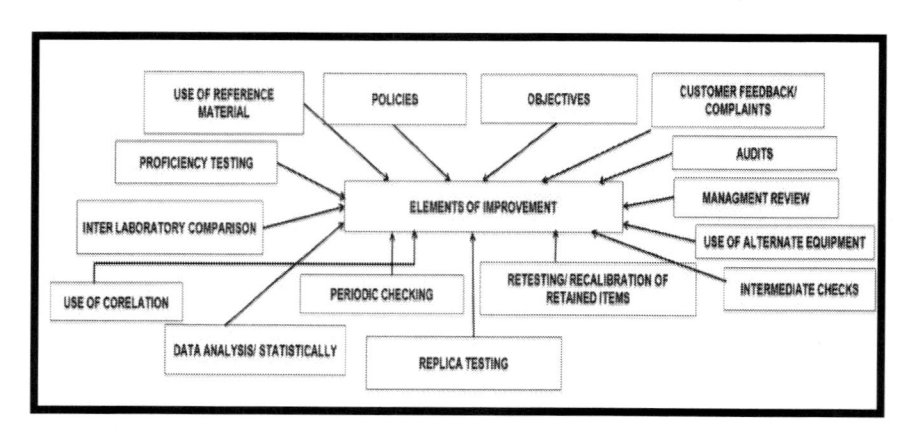

ELEMENT OF IMPROVEMENT

35. VARIOUS METHODS FOR IMPROVEMENT

- Use of reference material or standard reference materials.
- Intermediate checks.
- Retesting or recalibration of retained items.
- Replicate test or calibration.
- Periodic checking of measuring equipment.
- Use of alternative equipment.
- Uses of correlation between different characteristics of an item.
- Participate in inter laboratory comparisons
- Participation in proficiency testing.
- Statistical analysis of the data.

36. ANALYSIS OF DATA FOR CONTINUAL IMPROVEMENT

The analysis of data related to the following can be carried out:

- Key performance indicators, objectives, management programmes
- Customer feedback, complaints, orders and satisfaction surveys
- Conformity to product specifications, rejections, reworks, acceptance under concession,
- Characteristics and trends of processes and products

- Performance of externally provided products, services and processes
- Breakdown record of machineries and equipment
- Measurement and monitoring data.

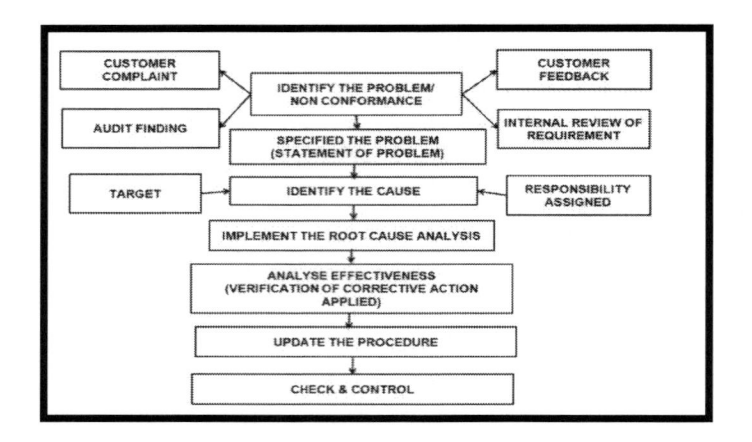

Root Cause Analysis Flow chart

37. TOOLS USED FOR IMPROVEMENT

Improvement is the basic premise of ISO. Following are the ways for improvement in the laboratory processes:

- Quality objectives and its performance report.
- Failure mode effect analysis.
- Internal audit
- Management review meeting
- Benchmarking.
- Statistical process control (SPC).
- 5S (sort, store, shine, standardize and sustain).

38. CORRECTIVE ACTION (8.7)

Action that is taken to eliminate the cause of the existence non conformity is called corrective action. It is an action to avoid recurrence of an event.

- When any non-conformity observed in the system:
    - Take corrective action.
    - Non conformity need not recur.
    - Implement the action needed.
    - Review the effectiveness.
    - Consider the risk and opportunities.
    - Explore any changes required in working.
    - Monitor the corrective action for effectiveness.

EVIDENCE REQUIRED:

Maintain the records of:

- Nature of non- conformity observed.
- Root cause analysis.
- Corrective action taken.
- Authorisation of person for taking corrective actions.
- Review of corrective actions taken.
- Risk and opportunities involved in taking the corrective actions.
- Time required for taking the corrective actions.
- Person authorising for corrective actions.
- Person responsible for resumption of work.

39. INTERNAL AUDIT (8.8)

Internal audit: Inspection and verification of effectiveness of system

Internal audits:

- Can be technical audits, process audits, and product/service audits.
- Helps a company/organization to channelize, synchronize and regularize the activity/operations.

The audit structuring involves:

- Audit criterion.
- Audit frequency.
- Audit methodology.
- Auditor qualification and experience.
- Audit plan.
- Auditing procedure.
- Audit reporting.
- Audit compliances.

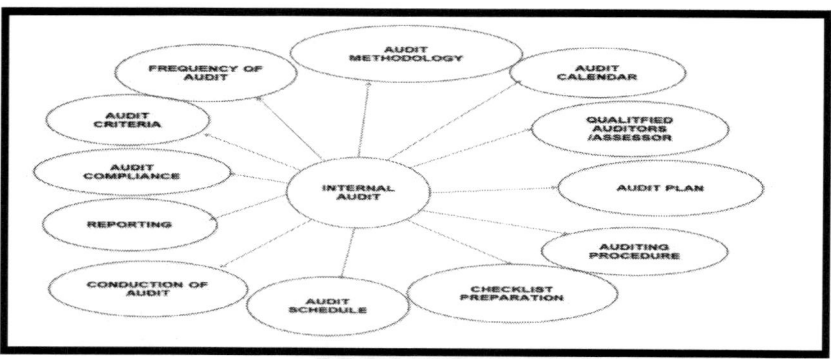

PROCESS OF INTERNAL AUDIT

40. GUIDELINES FOR CONDUCTION OF INTERNAL AUDIT

Internal audits to be conducted to check the extent to which the compliance to standard, statutory and regulatory requirements is maintained.

For conducting internal audit:

- Form the audit team.
- Train the team for ISO 17025:2017 internal audit.
- Prepare internal audit procedure along with internal audit formats.
- Decide the frequency of audit and prepare the plan.
- Prepare the schedule (time table) of internal audit.
- Conduct the audit as per schedule.
- Prepare audit report specifying the audit findings
- Comply all the audit findings.
- Prepare the audit summery report.
- Discuss the compliance status in management review meeting.

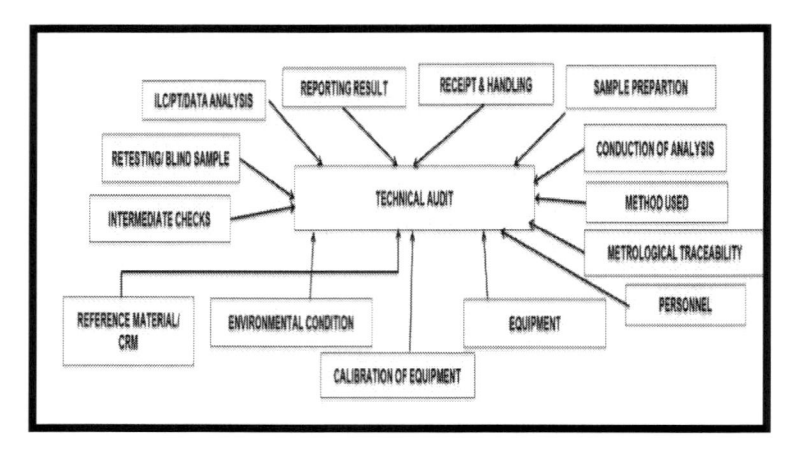

Technical Audit

EVIDENCE REQUIRED:

- List of internal auditors.
- Training certificate copy of internal auditors.
- Internal audit calendar.
- Internal audit schedule.
- Internal audit observation sheet.
- Internal audit summary
- Non- conformance.
- Corrective action taken.

41. MANAGEMENT REVIEWS (8.9)

Management review meeting is the meeting that is schedule and conducted at regular intervals along with the top management to discuss the performance of the laboratory quality management system and to take corrective action wherever necessary.

Following needs to be ensured related to MRM:

- Review by Top management of the laboratory.

Appointment and presence of members of management committee.

Conduction at planned intervals

Agenda of management review meeting as per standard and lab requirements.

Date, time, venue of management review meeting.

Communications for management review meeting within defined time frame before schedule of management review meeting.

Responsibility for issuing the circular and preparation of minutes.

- The reports, data, information etc. to be available with each member of meeting while coming to meeting.

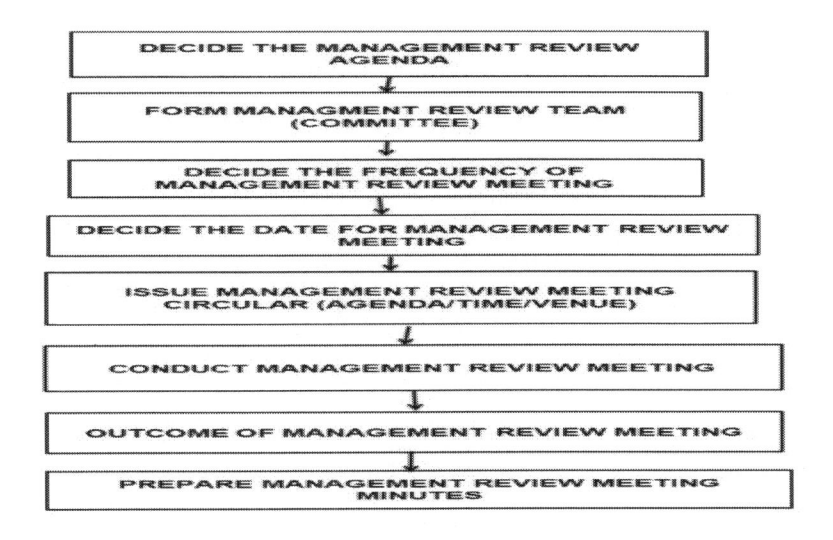

```
DECIDE THE MANAGEMENT REVIEW AGENDA
          ↓
FORM MANAGMENT REVIEW TEAM (COMMITTEE)
          ↓
DECIDE THE FREQUENCY OF MANAGEMENT REVIEW MEETING
          ↓
DECIDE THE DATE FOR MANAGEMENT REVIEW MEETING
          ↓
ISSUE MANAGEMENT REVIEW MEETING CIRCULAR (AGENDA/TIME/VENUE)
          ↓
CONDUCT MANAGEMENT REVIEW MEETING
          ↓
OUTCOME OF MANAGEMENT REVIEW MEETING
          ↓
PREPARE MANAGEMENT REVIEW MEETING MINUTES
```

PROCESS OF MANAGEMENT REVIEW MEETING

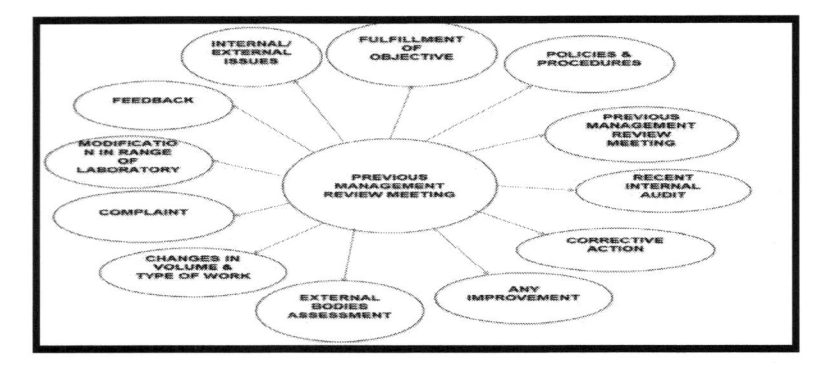

AGENDA OF MANAGEMENT REVIEW MEETING

Agenda of the meeting:

- Changes in internal and external issues those are relevant to the laboratory.
- Risk analysis and management
- Fulfilment of objectives.
- Suitability of policies and procedures.
- Status of actions from previous management reviews.
- Outcome of recent internal and external audits.
- Corrective actions.
- Assessment by external bodies including customers
- Changes in the volume and type of the work.
- Changes in the range of laboratory activities.
- Customer and personnel feedback and actions.
- Complaints from interested parties.
- Process performance
- Results and trends of quality assurance activities
- Training of personnel
- Calibration, Proficiency testing, Inter lab comparison results
- Effectiveness of Improvement.

Evidence Required:

Record of:

- Formation of Management committee.
- Circular of meeting.
- Minutes of management review meeting.
- Actions discussed and required.
- Corrective action planned and taken
- Target date for actions planned
- Responsibility delegation
- Time required for completion.
- Verification of Corrective action.
- Resource required for planned actions.

Author's profile

Dr. R. R. LAKHE

Dr. R. R. LAKHE, is presently working as Director, Shreyas Quality Management System, SQMS, Nagpur. He is registered Sr. Consultant for ISO9001-2015 QMS and ISO 17025 LQMS with Quality Council of India and is recognized Lean consultant.

He persues both academic & professional interest. Deeply interested in learning, he has completed, in addition to his PhD in Industrial Engineering, Masters in Management, Sociology, Public Administration, Training & Development. He is Qualified Lead Assessor for ISO9001 QMS, ISO14001EMS,ISO 50001ENMS & OHSAS 18001. He is Master Black Belt Six Sigma.

Academically he has guided 14 PhD scholar in both Nagpur & Amaravati University. He is member of RRC in Mumbai University. He is Co-author of Two books; `Handbook of Total Quality Management' & `Total Quality Management for Service Sector' (Published by JAICO Publication). He is reviewer for International Journals published by Emerald, Taylor & Francis, Inderscience etc. He is on advisory boards of number of engineering colleges.

Professionally he has provided training & consultancy to more than 200 organisations at national & International level on various performance improvement aspects such as Quality Award, ISO9000, ISO14000, ISO50001 ENMS,OHSAS1 8000, ISO22000,ISO17025, 5 S, Kaizen, Six Sigma, NABL accreditation, FAMI-QS,BIFMA.

Dr.Rakesh L Shrivastava

Dr.Rakesh L Shrivastava, is currently working as Professor of Mechanical Engineering in Yashwantrao Chavan College of Engineering, Nagpur, India. He has done PhD in Mechanical engineering and also completed MBA. He is Lead Auditor for ISO9001:2015 and ISO50001 EnMS and has conducted audits of various orgnisations. He is Master Black Belt Six Sigma and has guided 8 research scholars for PhD. He is proficient researcher, trainer, auditor and consultant in Quality management. He is active member of various professional associations like Institution of Engineers (I).

Dr. Sapan Kumar Ganguly

- **Dr. Sapan Kumar Ganguly** is presently working as a professor & Head of the Department of Mechanical Engineering in Bhilai Institute of Technology. He has more than 30 years of experience in mechanical engineering and has carried out research in Measurement of Uncertainty. He has life membership of Indian Society for Technical Education, New Delhi.

He has been associated with many academic bodies such as Chairman BOS (Mechanical Engg.), CSVTU, Bhilai, Ex. Member of Executive council in CSVTU, Bhilai (CG),Member of Board of Studies in Mechanical, Production, Industrial Engineering , Nagpur University, Nagpur(MS), Member of Faculty of Engineering Nagpur University, Nagpur (MS).). He has to his credit more than 20 papers in International journals of repute and more than 5 papers in National Journal & conferences. He has delivered several lectures on areas such as TQM, ISO 9000, Six Sigma, Uncertainty of measurement and Lab Quality Management System.

M M Naveed

M M Naveed is presently working as a Senior consultant for Laboratory Quality Management System, ISO, Food Management System, FAMI-QS with Shreyas Quality Management System, Nagpur. He is post graduate in Microbiology and Lead Auditor for ISO 22000, Food Safety Management System. He has total working experience of 20 years at various capacities in various organizations and has also worked as a Quality Control Incharge in Kingdom of Saudi Arabia. He has provided training and consultancy related to laboratory quality management system, measurement uncertainty, Integrated management system to various organizations.

Printed in Great Britain
by Amazon